Changing your thou
winning, losing, failure & determination

UNDEFEATABLE
CONQUERING SELF-DEFEAT

Tiana Sanchez
co-author of *Leaders in Pearls*

Undefeatable

Conquering Self-Defeat

Copyright © 2013

Printed in the United States of America

Book Cover Design by: Monish Subherwal, Graphic Designer

Artist and Design Expert: Jahn Evans

Red Vintage Gloves Image supplied by: Getty Images

Published by Professional Woman Publishing, LLC
www.pwnbooks.com

TABLE OF CONTENTS

TABLE OF CONTENTS

Dedication

I thank God for blessing me with the ability to inspire others through writing. I dedicate this book to my husband and children and thank them for their unwavering support and love. A special dedication to my sister who will forever be the "undefeated one" in my book. You will inspire others in dark times and encourage them to push through adversity.

FOREWORD

I encourage you to read Tiana Sanchez's book as it is powerful in conquering self-pity, self-doubt, and unbelief. She's calling on us to refuse to live a defeated life.

In this book, *Undefeatable*, Tiana says defeat is a toxic state of mind that blocks us from achieving our goals and dreams and keeps us stuck in the "defeated zone." She challenges our perception of failure and defeat and states, "you may fail, but you will not be defeated!"

I know first-hand as a two-time cancer conqueror that obstacles can come into your life that challenge your faith and cause fear to enter into our lives. Tiana boldly identifies the many types of fear that keeps us from moving forward and how that fear hinders our progress. I encourage you to take the time to complete the exercises in the book to get clear on your areas of "defeat."

Tiana is brilliant at helping you uncover the real reasons behind your defeated mind-set. Each chapter is designed to expand your mind set, increase you courage and inspire you to change your life.

Tiana gets raw and personal as she shares a true story of remarkable determination and faith. A story that will empower, encourage and renew your faith. I have been blessed by this book and encourage any person who has ever failed at something and given up hope to read this book. As a Speaker, Life Coach and Author, Tiana is a messenger of hope, an agent of transformation and a positive powerful force on the planet that will change millions of lives.

—Les Brown, *Author, Speaker, Speech Coach*

INTRODUCTION

"Material possessions, winning scores, and great reputations are meaningless in the eyes of the Lord, because He knows what we really are and that is all that matters." —John Wooden

Two things happened to me that prompted me to write this book. Both were life changing circumstances that changed my perspective on what it means to be UNDEFEATED. We tend to view ourselves as either "winners" or "losers" in this game of life. We don't get the job we want so we're losers. We get laid off from a job and we feel defeated. YOU ARE NOT DEFEATED! What matters most is how you pick yourself up and overcome that temporary set-back by not allowing that circumstance to define you. Winning is not about how much money you have in your bank account. It's not how many friends you have or your class and status. And if you lose at something, that doesn't mean defeat. We are so much more blessed than we ever could imagine if we measure our "wins" and "losses" not by our bank accounts but instead by what's in our character. *Teaching moment.*

This book is designed for your personal and professional development. Inside, there are tools and exercises that have helped me overcome many challenges and unbeatable circumstances. Weaved in the pages are stories that will encourage you and empower you to see yourself as a WINNER at all times. Whether you are an entrepreneur, athlete, teacher, CEO, student, Coach, or professional you will gain new perspective on winning, losing, failure and defeat. These are the building blocks to changing your thoughts and perceptions about winning and losing, failure and defeat, in your life, career, and relationships. Conquer the defeated mind-set. We all have felt a sense of defeat in our lives and I'm here to tell you that you may fail, heck you may fail several times but what you will not be is DEFEATED!

CHAPTER 1

THE FIGHT WITHIN

"It is impossible to win the race unless you venture to run, impossible to win the victory unless you dare to battle." —Richard M. DeVos

Why do some of us feel defeated in our careers, business and relationships? When I think of defeat I think of someone getting knocked down, crushed, conquered and unable to move. Unable to bring themselves out of a deep dark place of hopelessness and despair. For most us when we think of being defeated, it's a permanent place or position. I believe it stops people dead in their tracks. It's the hopelessness one feels when one doesn't succeed in an area of their life and they feel like a "failure." If you don't get that job you applied for or that promotion you wanted you "failed" in your career. If you experience financial difficulties, lose all of your possessions and are at your wits end, you failed as a provider and therefore feel defeated. Failure is not defeat. **Failure** is a temporary set-back when one has not achieved an expected result or outcome. The key is when we fail, we pick ourselves up and continue onward with determination. **Defeat** is allowing yourself to wallow in self-pity thereby deactivating your drive and ambition. Failure is inevitable. It's part of growing. Some of the best inventions were the result of a failed attempt the first time. One must try and try again and never give up. You may fail but you must not allow yourself to become defeated.

Rags to Enrichment

Zero was the number in my bank account. I can recall no job, no real clients, a family to clothe and feed and a mortgage to pay. This is a snapshot of my situation after being laid off and starting my coaching practice. If you're thinking this is one of those "rags to riches" stories let me stop you right there. This is not that kind of party. I am still overcoming in many areas I discuss. I'm still a work in progress and growing every day. It's not what happens to us that defines us, it's how we pick ourselves up and keep going.

How many of you have faced an empty bank account? If you think of how the number zero is shaped, it's very telling. There's a big hole in the center, an empty space of nothingness. That's how some of us feel when we have zero, nothing. When I noticed the bank accounts depleting, it concerned me greatly. I took a huge risk starting a business during a difficult time in the economy. It was at the time where Coaching practices were popping up everywhere which made it difficult for me to set myself apart from others who had been practicing a lot longer than me. But I was determined, passionate and believed that this was my mission in life. I still believe that. It was a risk I was willing to take and so I stepped out on faith.

What's a risk without challenges? The risk was pursuing my career in coaching and the challenge was doing this successfully without a consistent flow of income. This was a temporary set-back. Monthly bills and budgeting took on a whole new meaning. I cut costs or "trimmed the fat" on unnecessary expenses. But there were some expenses that *were* necessary. The mortgage was coming due one month in the spring and I didn't know how it was going to get paid. A month before, I had applied for a program that offered assistance to homeowners suffering a hardship where their home was undervalued due to the recession. If approved, my expenses would be significantly reduced. Bringing in a consistent income at the time was infrequent because I just started a new business. It takes time, money and resources for an effective start-up and entrepreneur. Clients and money were on the to-do-list but not checked off yet. I applied for the program and waited. I waited with hopefulness right up until a week before the mortgage was due. I received a letter in the mail one week before the mortgage was due stating that I was approved for this program. What a blessing! Throughout that whole time of not knowing and facing an empty bank account, the important piece to take away is that I didn't give up hope. I didn't allow my circumstances and the temporary set-back to defeat me.

Show and Tell

There are times when we think life is unfair. We ask ourselves, "Why is this happening to me?" We start to feel sorry for ourselves and welcome self-pity. We may never know why things "happen" to us but it's up to you to decide how you are going to get through it. I'm faced with the same challenges as everyone else. I'm just like you. I *am* you! Every morning I wake up, I'm prepared for whatever challenges lie ahead. I know that I won't be given a challenge that is more than I can handle. I greet the day with a positive attitude, read a scripture or affirmation and put my feet on the ground and GET TO IT! It's not always easy but I'm a fighter. It's because of this internal fight and drive that I will never be defeated and neither will you!

Here's what I'm not going to do in this book and that is sell you something. If something is of value, it will sell itself. It's a SHOW and TELL. I want to show you through activities how you can become undefeatable and tell you what works for me. When you get to the point when you feel the world is on your shoulders and crashing down on you and you feel hopeless, look to the words in this book for encouragement. When you feel you have no more fight left in you, remember you have to "activate" that internal fight within that is lying dormant. Whether you have a little or a lot, you are not immune to life's trials and tribulations. You can have an abundance and one day have it all taken away. How will you go on? Tap into that fight within and come out of it a winner!

There are obstacles that you will face and have faced in your life. How will you overcome them? Are you still fighting the good fight? I want you take a hard and honest look at yourself and recognize the areas of defeat that you have allowed to enter your space. Notice where you are lacking in your career, business, relationships and health and ask yourself are you lacking because you gave into defeat?

Ask yourself...

> *What areas have I considered "over and done with",*
> *incomplete, unfinished?*
> *Have I given up on relationships?*
> *Am I settling in my career?*
> *Do I know what it really means to win, succeed, win, lose or fail?*

We are caught up in a defeated mind-set when in reality it's nothing more than a temporary set-back. When you look at yourself, what are you doing to improve your situation? Are you wallowing in self-pity? Are you allowing the temporary set-back to prevent you from moving forward? Are you allowing toxic relationships into your life? Am I touching a nerve yet?

My goal is to catch you and get you on track before you enter the "defeated zone." Once you enter the defeated zone you experience hopelessness, powerlessness, despair, emptiness, loneliness, and unhappiness. To conquer self-defeat, you must tap into your internal resources, which I refer to as weapons, to help you combat and become an overcomer. It requires a shift in your thinking, practical action steps, effort and optimism. I'm speaking from the heart and from experience.

Born a Fighter

I grew up in a modest home with traditional, Christian upbringing with my Mom, Dad and two siblings. My Dad was a blue-collar worker and my Mom a domesticated wife (stay-at-home Mom). My Mom always said I was the stubborn baby. Born 8 lbs. to a woman 4 ft., 11 inches tall, I would say stubborn and heavy. I had sass and a smart mouth. Unafraid to speak and give my honest opinion. I challenged authority and was often called "ornery." A term southern folks used to describe a strong-willed child. Strong willed indeed. This served me well as a teenager and later as an adult.

With one working parent we had our fair share of financial struggles. I remember vividly going to the gas station and scraping up enough pennies to put gas in the car. We moved around a lot but even still, we never felt a sense of lack or felt "less-than." Of course there were things we wanted that we couldn't afford but we got over it and made the best of what we did have. I recall one Christmas we were really struggling financially and gifts that year were scarce. To make sure we didn't do without, my Mom arranged for the Salvation Army to bring us gifts that year. They showed up in a big Salvation Army truck and dropped off gifts for me and my two siblings. It took me a long time and having children of my own to realize how amazing that was. Imagining how my Mother must have felt not being able to provide for her children and instead of saying, "I give up" She found a way. It's not about the presents but the determination and not giving in to a moment of defeat. She didn't give up because of us.

I learned a great deal from that experience. As I grew up, my personal journey in life consumed many challenges. At age 16, I started working so that I could financially take care of myself. After the divorce of my parents, four years prior, times got even harder. I grew up quickly and became a responsible teenager. To relieve some of the burden off my Mom, I paid for my prom, braces and bought my first car. That experience fueled my internal drive and ambition and taught me that I have to go after what I want.

At age 17 I had worked my way up to Manager. Every company I ever worked for in the years to come would result in a manager-level or leadership-level position. Drive is a powerful thing! Drive is not void of challenges however and I had to face difficult times once again. As a young Manager, I faced ridicule, disrespect and prejudices about my ability to lead. I'm still standing.

At age 21 I was married and had my first child at age 22. I married young and you could say I was blinded by "love" or fooled by it. The marriage happened quickly and soon proved to be a toxic relationship. 18 months after we married, we separated and 18 months after that we divorced. Twenty-five, a single Mom and already divorced. You don't go into a relationship hoping it will fail. But fail it did. I have to admit, I felt like a loser. But what did I really lose? I *lost* the self-pity. I *lost* the feeling of powerlessness. I *lost* a bad marriage. I had to realize that what I lost wasn't worth me holding on to anyway. It wasn't what I lost but what I still had. I had my self-worth, my independence, my peace of mind. And I'm ok with that! I gained self-confidence and was a better person for it.

It took a long time and a lot of self-assessing, mistakes, and obstacles to understand this concept of winning, losing, failure and defeat. And just when you think it can't get any worse, sometimes it does. You must find that internal fight because the hits keep on coming!

Changing My Thoughts and Perceptions

Write down how your thoughts and perceptions on self-defeat have changed after reading this chapter.

CHAPTER 2

THE ONE DEGREE DIFFERENCE

"Adversity causes some men to break; others to break records"
—William Arthur Ward

Have you ever watched a race that was so close that they needed to slow down the replay to determine the winner? The difference could be a millisecond to determine who takes home the trophy. It's that one degree of difference that can have the greatest impact. Did you know that water reaches its boiling point at 212 degrees? Did you also know that the difference between hot water and boiling water is one degree? Did you know the difference between a .250 hitter in baseball and a .350 hitter is one extra hit every ten times at bat? But the difference between the earnings of .350 hitter compared to the .250 hitter are ten times greater. Did you know that the difference between a believer and non-believer is one mustard seed of faith? But the quality of enjoying life, in my opinion, is far more promising in a faith-filled person.

As a Coach, part of what I do is help my clients set and achieve clear and measurable goals. More importantly is the execution strategy that follows any effective goal. You've heard of the 7 Step Strategies and the "5 Tips to Success" type programs. There's nothing wrong with those programs. I personally have created programs just like that. Those programs are designed for people who like steps and processes. But, sometimes people can get caught up in the list of steps and feel overwhelmed by the entire process and never move past step one. So, I decided to simplify one's thinking by breaking down the process into one simple formula. I want to challenge you to make ONE significant shift in an area of your life. When you do that you will notice that small changes can have a BIG impact.

One significant shift can be powerful. If you embrace how one decision, one connection, one conversation or one bad attitude or negative thought can impact your situation drastically, then you might begin to understand the significance of one. We are all one opportunity away from our next opportunity. *Teaching moment.* This is powerful if you think about it. One great connection can be the difference between one opportunity or multiple opportunities. One person's words can be encouraging or discouraging, life-changing or life-damaging. One client can change your business, either good or bad.

As a business owner I can remember in the early stages of my business thinking all I need is that one break, that one client to take my business to the next level. The reality is that sometimes it works that way and sometimes it takes many small **one-time events** and tweaks that led up to a break. And sometimes it takes one moment of "perceived defeat" to knock some sense into us.

*"We are all one opportunity away
from our next opportunity."*

Perceived Defeat

If I were to tell you that I lost my job, had no known source of income, void of any degrees and had a famility to support, how would you react? Well, this was my story two years ago. Writing this down brings me back to that point in time as I remember how I felt. In one word I felt like a LOSER. I could feel the imprint of a big, bold letter 'L' branded on my forehead. But what did I really lose? I lost my job, yes. Money, yes. But, did that make me a loser, a has been? It was my perception of "winning" that allowed me to think I was a loser. I had entered into what I call, the "defeated zone." When you allow your circumstances to take over, you become powerless, hopeless and defeated.

But I wasn't defeated. I was going through a temporary set-back which can resemble defeat to most us. I call that illusion of defeat "perceived defeat." Perceived defeat is the illusion that you have been defeated because what you once deemed as "success" has been removed from your path. Now, if I had stayed in a "defeated mind-set" because I lost my job didn't have a degree and felt sorry for myself, and then it would not have been perceived defeat but real defeat. I had to focus on what I had and not what I didn't have. I experienced this perceived defeat but wasn't going to let it become my truth. I made ONE shift in my thinking and it was when I decided that **my EFFORT + my ACTIVITY + my ATTITUDE = a WIN**. If I proved to myself, not anyone else, that I put forth all of my effort and energy into improving my situation, take the necessary steps toward improving my situation and do this all with a positive attitude then I would always come out on top. One of my first experiences with this formula produced a big opportunity.

One Collaborative Effort

After losing my job I looked for many opportunities to collaborate and developing strategic alliances with organizations and individuals for the purpose of cross promotion and partnership. I realized my skills would be needed in various organizations and for people looking to develop specific skills that would increase their chances for career advancement. I diligently sought out individuals seeking a new career path and organizations with a "promote from within" culture that wanted to invest in their employees' development. Sound easy so far, right? So where does one go to seek out CEO's and professionals? Where else but the mega-hub of professional connections, LinkedIn (which has since proved to be a viable resource for my business). What also worked well was meeting them in *their* "space." So I joined groups, associations, and attended exclusive meetings.

One Exclusive Activity

The intent heading into these CEO meetings was 3-fold: suit up, show up and shut up. *Teaching moment.* A mantra shared from a multi-millionaire friend. One of the best words of advice I've received to date. Which means, look the part, be present and listen! If, during this event I walked away with ONE quality connection then it was worth my time. No loser here!

One man seated near me overheard my "pitch" about helping others develop specific skills that would increase their chances of career advancement. "I think colleges and universities would be a good fit for what you do," he said There's a group of CEO's that meet once a month on a campus at a local University and I think you should attend." Colleges? Universities? That wasn't on my agenda. Whether or not it was in the plan, it was an opportunity that I wasn't going to pass up especially since I was recently unemployed. I wasn't exactly sure where this was headed, but I was willing to move forward, one connection and activity at a time. I wanted that win!

One Assertive Attitude

There's nothing quite like walking into a room filled with seasoned, white collared men in business suits when you're a relatively young, black woman to get you questioning whether or not you made the right decision. After arriving I shortly realized that perhaps this wasn't the meeting for me. BUT, things don't always appear the way we envision or happen as we would like them to. Assertively, I connected with an individual who was interested in learning more about what I do as a Coach. Well this is awesome, I thought and scheduled a chat offline that would end with an invitation to participate in a live group coaching session where I was brought in as the Subject Matter Expert.

One Big Win for Me!

That ONE session led to more opportunities than I could have ever imagined. The "big win" was shifting my thought to "why not" instead of "why?". Following the initial session it was evident that I had stumbled upon something in the educational arena which was a far cry from the financial industry where I had left. Ironically, here I was without a degree, collaborating at a prestigious college and helping college students with coaching and career development plans. It was making a small but significant shift in my thought process, not allowing a perceived defeat to become an actual defeat and putting forth the right amount of effort, coupled with activities and displaying an assertive attitude. This is the recipe for creating opportunities and it begins with a small shift."

What Happens if the Shift You Make Isn't Enough

Water becomes hot at 212 degrees. Try cooking spaghetti at 211 degrees and see what happens. A big, sticky unflattering mess is the end result. Water needs to be boiling at just the right temperature to produce the Italian masterpiece known as spaghetti. Have you ever noticed that the instructions on a box of rice specifically require a "rolling boil" before adding the rice to the pot? What happens when you try to add dry rice to hot, not boiling, water? It takes longer, the texture changes, and flat out doesn't taste good. This is not a cook book or recipe for making great pasta and rice. Remember, that one degree of difference can have a major impact on an outcome. *Teaching moment.* The boiling point is the place in time when you activate your ambition and drive. Those are two necessary ingredients to overcome a defeated mind-set. Look at it this way. You'll get this, I promise.

When we strive for success and set goals we're creating a roadmap or recipe for future outcomes. The goals must be clearly defined, have a purpose, aligned with your values and beliefs and have an execution strategy. But that's not enough. Oftentimes this "recipe" will call for a little something extra. Cooks, culinary gurus and chefs call it love. Love for cooking. Love is in the details, right. The little something extra we need is determination (boiling water), drive and ambition with a dash of perseverance. Without the right amount of determination and drive, your goals will just be words on a paper and thoughts of success will be an unreachable goal.

"The boiling point is the place in time when you activate your ambition and drive."

A Defeated Mind

Your drive cannot be lackluster or weak. Executing goals with weak determination or drive is a recipe for defeat. Notice I didn't say failure, Failure will happen to most of us but that's part of the process. If you want a great story of failure just reflect on Thomas Edison's story. According to history books about Thomas Edison, it took over 10,000 attempts before he invented the light bulb. So, ultimately, he failed thousands of times before he succeeded. But at the end of the day, he did succeed! Defeat, again is allowing yourself to wallow in self-pity thereby deactivating your drive and ambition. It's giving up hope. A defeated mind-set is a toxic one. *Teaching moment.* Don't allow yourself to get into the "defeated zone." Instead, get a determined mind. The "defeated zone" is the place where you deactivate your drive and determination and replace it with FEAR, regret, excuses and hopelessness. Embrace failure as part of the process. Failure does not equal defeat. Shift your thinking and get out of the defeated mind-set.

"A defeated mind-set is a toxic one."

Chapter Takeaway: *What's one degree or shift you can make today in your career, relationship, finances that will have the biggest impact?*

Changing My Thoughts and Perceptions

Write down how your thoughts and perceptions on self-defeat have changed after reading this chapter.

CHAPTER 3

DEFEAT IS
IMPOSSIBLE

"Defeat is impossible if you always look at the possibilities and not the limitations." —Tiana Sanchez

Possibilities vs. Limitations

How would it feel if you set ONE clear objective at the start of every day? How easy would that be? Most of us could accomplish one objective a day, right? What about 20 objectives a day? Whew! Well, let me let you in on little secret. Most of us average a 50% completion rate on daily tasks or goals. In some cases, a 33% completion rate. Now, this is merely my opinion based on my 15 years' experience managing others. There's no hard core data in this book that supports my opinion but you can look at your task list and tell me I'm wrong. So, why are we creating tasks that we don't complete and make us feel like losers and poor time managers? Are we lazy, poor at managing our time or caught up in the task itself and not looking at it as a significant part of the expected outcome or results.

When I explored the thought of starting my own business, I was afraid. I had never owned a business before nor did I know where to begin. So I started with one set goal at a time. Get a name for the business. Create a Business Plan. Get a license. Get a website. Build strategic alliances. Get a team of people smarter than me to help me avoid mistakes. YEAH! Each objective was achieved one at a time with a clear purpose and understanding of the expected outcome. Each goal was a significant achievement so I made certain to celebrate. By celebrating, I approached each new goal with determination and looked forward to the next goal. Again, it's changing your mindset. Once you begin to look at the possibilities and not the limitations you get clear on the purpose and develop a new found commitment to the goal. This requires that one-degree shift in one's thinking.

Perseverance is Possible

If every person who invented a new product called it quits each time they ran into a roadblock, where would we be with technology, automobiles, etc.? If they allowed that one moment of doubt and insecurity to reside in their thoughts, do you think they would have persevered? All it takes is one thought of doubt, or someone telling you, "you can't do it", and a limiting belief begins to manifest inside of you. From that moment on, that's all you will focus on. How many of you know it's so much easier to believe the bad stuff than the good stuff? In my opinion, I believe we have low expectations of ourselves and other people which makes it easier to believe the bad stuff. How do we shift from being negative seekers to positive believers? Faith!

Faith is Possible

I am a woman of faith and my faith is tested every day. And I can honestly say, I don't always pass my test. I have to work at it just like anything else in my life. I have to practice trusting and believing even in the most trying situations. When you practice a faith-filled lifestyle, you:

- Look beyond the circumstances that are in front of you

- Visualize the outcome in your favor

- Trust, trust, and trust some more

- See the troubled waters but you press on anyway

- Celebrate where you are because although you haven't arrived to your destination, you have faith that you will get there!

Success is Possible

Success is used loosely in this book because we all have a different and oftentimes skewed definition of success. Success, to me is never giving up. It represents a host of other things but mostly never giving into defeat. Success is incremental, celebrating the small achievements of a greater goal. I'm going to show you how to get comfortable patting yourself on the back. Celebrating the small wins is easier than you imagine.

I learned this lesson in the early stages of dating my husband. I had been in previous relationships whereas he had only one serious relationship. So I had an expectation of what was going to happen in our relationship based on past experiences. Sound familiar? We often approach things in our career, business and life in general with this type of antiquated way of thinking. We go in with a pre-determined idea of what success is supposed to look like. Well, I was no exception to the rule.

This was my version of a successful courtship: (1) meet, (2) date, (3) date some more, (4) date exclusively, (5) say "I love you", (6) propose, and (7) marry. In that order. It was a mere 3 months and I was ready for the "ring" talk. Okay, well maybe not that short but definitely within the first 6 months. The problem with that is he had a different plan: (1) meet, (2) talk, (3) date, (4) get to know each other, (5) spend time together, (6) hang out, (7) "I like you", (8) travel, (9) introduce to friends, (10) introduce to family, (11) travel some more, (12) continue to date, (13) "I think I love you", (14) "I love you", (15) "will you marry me", (16) more travel, (17) marry. Whew! I got the picture rather quickly when I told him I love him and he didn't say it back. I knew he was different. A "one size fits all" mentality doesn't work with people. *Teaching Moment.* We need to approach our relationships and other areas in our life with the right intentions. So I celebrated every small step in our relationship. It was a win in my book. Ten years and two kids later, I can honestly say, SUCCESS!

"Celebrate the small wins."

Maybe relationships aren't an area where you're experiencing the greatest struggle of success, winning and losing. What if weight is the issue? Did I hit a nerve with that one? A large percentage of people today struggle with their health and weight. I'm not proving to have a health plan or diet for weight loss but I would like to challenge your way of thinking for a moment. Let's say, you needed to lose 30 pounds. How would you approach that challenge? Do you already count yourself as being defeated before you've even begun the fight? Are you planning on waiting until you lose all 30 pounds before you celebrate and relish in your success? If that's you, you're cheating yourself out of joy. Here's how you should approach the challenge according to someone who needed to lose 30 pounds after the birth of her second child – ME!

Get Determined

Make it up in your mind from the beginning that you are going to do this! Start ridding yourself of temptations, toxic people, and unhealthy environments.

Visualize the Outcome

How you see yourself at the end of your journey is key. What do you look like? What are you wearing? If you can't see your outcome, then you don't truly believe you can achieve.

Get Uncomfortable

You haven't arrived until you're out of your comfort zone. I refused to buy any new clothes so guess what? When I wanted to go out with friends and couldn't fit into my favorite pair of jeans, I was angry. Anger worked to my advantage because it pushed me.

Attach a Reward

"Every five pounds I lose, buy a new pair of shoes." That was my daily mantra that encouraged me to rid myself of that extra weight.

A small goal, big reward. I treated myself every time I achieved that five pound milestone. It made the process fun and exciting. I had something to look forward to and it seemed more attainable.

Celebrate the Small Wins

"Incremental success." Get comfortable with that concept. Success isn't a one-time event but several small achievements or "wins." Focus on that one pound that you lost and rejoice in that small success. You lose one more pound, celebrate again. Another pound, keep celebrating.

What about in business. You book one client. CELEBRATE!. Soon your "one" clients will have turned into many. You write the first chapter of your 300 page book. CELEBRATE! It's starting with one and celebrating in that moment. There's a simple equation that I mentioned at the beginning of this book that will help you. Effort + Activity + Attitude = a WIN. When you begin to celebrate the small success in your life, you begin to feel/experience:

- Renewed commitment to the goal

- Renewed focus

- Energized

- Hopeful about the future

- Determined to see it all the way through

- Belief in yourself and the process

- Confident

- Unstoppable

Effort – The Webster Dictionary defines effort as the mental of physical energy that is exerted in order to achieve a purpose.

- Determination

- Energy

Activity – Is the act of doing. It's taking your energy and putting it into motion. Activities are the movements, steps that we take to reach a goal or destination.

- Action

- Motion

- Doing

Confident (can-do) Attitude – A confident attitude is an attitude of pure certainty. An individual who believes in not only him/herself but is certain that the outcome will be favorable has a confident attitude.

- Positive point of view

- Positive outlook

- Positive affirmations

- Optimistic

"Success isn't a one-time event but several small achievements or "wins."

...and when you do that, the results will come. Don't allow the what if's to affect your success.

Limitations are Hindrances

Do you still feel inhibited by limitations and focused on what you haven't attained instead of looking at the possibilities of what you could achieve? This limited way of thinking hinders a lot of people from putting their feet to the pavement and taking action toward new possibilities. Life requires us to take a certain amount of risks and quite honestly, I think that frightens most of us. We get consumed by the "what if's." "What if it doesn't work?" What if nobody approves?" "What if I fail?" Remember, failure is not defeat. Failure is a temporary set-back and comes with the territory of taking risks. We all experience temporary set-backs. What's important is that you took the risk despite of the "what if's." You have to make a decision in that moment to rid yourself of negative thinking and sow positive "seeds."

A Seed of Possibility

Planting a seed in this book is a metaphor for what you put forth in the world, the seed. The "harvest" is the *product* of what you put out, the sown seed. To reap the benefits of a good harvest takes careful thought, preparation, the right tools, the right timing, and a solid foundation. There is a scripture in the bible in II Corinthians 9:6, "…whoever sows sparingly will also reap sparingly, and whoever sows bountifully will also reap bountifully." I like this passage because it's giving you the recipe for a successful harvest.

A Seed of Prosperity

Did you know that you plant seeds every day? They're in the words you say, the things you do and the people you help. Have you ever said or heard someone else say, "I can't do this." Well, you just planted a seed of defeat. You've lost the battle before you've even begun. Conversely if you have you ever said to someone, "You *can* do this!" You've planted a seed of encouragement within that person. We may never fully know the impact our words have on others but I promise you it makes a difference. We have to be mindful of what we say and what we're putting out in the world. WORDS ARE POWERFUL!

The Manifestation of Your Harvest

Our words and actions manifest itself in many ways. You may not know the impact your words and actions have on others but you will certainly feel the impact when it's about you. A simple phrase like, "I can't do this," can hold you back from many opportunities. You're speaking limiting words and not possible ones. *Teaching moment.* If you say you can't, then you won't. There was a quote that resonated with me a few years ago, "*If you think you can or think you can't, you're right.*" What are you saying about yourself and your abilities?

Look at it this way. If farming was your way of life, you would have to decide what seeds to sow that will produce the biggest return or harvest to survive over the course of a year. The seeds you plant support your family, provide income and help the community where you live. There is careful thought in determining what seeds to sow that again will produce the biggest harvest. Each seed represents life, food, sustainability, income and multiple opportuntieis. So as a farmer you are going to nurture each seed to reach its full potential.

What does your future harvest look like? This depends on your needs and that will determine the harvest that you will reap. Some of you have financial, spiritual, relationship and career needs. As you plant those figurative seeds you *will* see a harvest! But it doesn't happen overnight. It requires the right amount of effort, purposeful activity and the right attitude.

Naysayers – The Defeated Ones

Not everybody will see your vision and be supportive. Be aware of those that will try to steal your harvest, your joy. I recall a friend of mine telling me flat out that, "I would fail." He didn't understand why I left a "promising" career in the financial industry to pursue this coaching thing. Truth be told, he wasn't the only one who felt that way but he was the only one who said it aloud. When he made that statement he reiterated that it was his duty as a "friend" to give it to me straight and tell me the truth. But it was *his* truth, not mine. Rid yourself of the naysayers that believe you don't have what it takes. Be diligent in sowing seeds and the harvest will come.

Stay away from the naysayers and out of the "defeated zone" by protecting your future harvest and…

- **Committing** to the work needed to bring forth the outcome

- **Planning** purposeful steps along the way

- **Think Positively** throughout difficult "seasons" or circumstances

- **Visualize** to help see the bigger picture

- **Set a Solid foundation** or "good" soil that will develop the seed(s)

- **Cultivate** and live a life of purpose and possibility!

Chapter Takeaway: *What's one "seed of possibility" that you can sow today?*

Changing My Thoughts and Perceptions

Write down how your thoughts and perceptions on self-defeat have changed after reading this chapter.

CHAPTER 4

THE FEAR OF DEFEAT OR (DEFEATED FEAR)

"Fear is why most people don't pursue their passion; they are afraid of failing. But, what's worse than failing is the regret of never having tried at all." —Tiana Sanchez

What is that ONE thing that's really holding you back and keeping you in the "defeated zone?" People create 101 reasons or excuses as to why they didn't accomplish what they set out to accomplish. They make excuses why they aren't pursing their dreams, career aspirations, financial freedom, a healthier lifestyle, or peace in their relationships. In my experience, there's always an underlying issue and it's usually FEAR. Fear is like a cancer to people, paralyzing them from moving forward. They remain stuck in their situation unable to move beyond their circumstances. Clients will tell me many reasons why they're stuck: finances, education, resources, support, etc. What it really boils down to is that they are lacking an internal drive, confidence, determination and ambition.

I spent years in management working in a myriad of industries and with all different types of people. I recall working with a young woman who had remained in her current position for about 12 years. She had developed a good reputation within the company, was skilled and proficient, highly knowledgeable but in my opinion was too comfortable. After working with her for a while I strongly encouraged her to break out of her comfort zone and challenge herself. Through conversation, she openly expressed that taking on a new role was too "risky" and that the greater responsibility and uncertainty, quite frankly, frightened her. Complacency became the norm. In my opinion I believed that it was fear of failure and stepping into "uncertainty" that was holding her back. She had all of the qualifications to transition into a senior manager position but she feared the greater responsibility and lacked the confidence to get "unstuck" and move forward in her career. FEAR was holding her back and she remained in that position throughout her tenure with the company.

Another young woman I worked with, in a similar situation took a different path. When given the opportunity to excel and move forward she took the "bull by the horns" and forged ahead. This young woman was also in a Supervisors role for many, many years and displayed earlier signs of complacency. The same role, with the same risks was presented to her but she decided that now was as good of a time as any to take a leap of faith. To this day, she continues to excel in her role as a leader, taking on new challenges and leaving room for new possibilities.

Four Common Types of Fear

What is it about FEAR? In the first example the "one" thing holding her back was FEAR: fear of failure, fear of taking risks, fear of new responsibility and fear of uncertainty. I believe one of these four types of fears that I'm going to describe prevents most of us from moving forward and keeps us stuck in the defeated zone.

1. **Fear of Failure** – This is the number one reason why people do not succeed. Napoleon Hill once described failure as a "temporary defeat." I view a temporary defeat as a temporary set-back or life lesson which shouldn't be feared but accepted as part of maturing. I like to refer to it as "perceived defeat." The illusion that you have been defeated because what you once deemed as "successful" has been removed from your path. "Fail your way to the top" is another phrase I've heard articulated by many business owners and prominent figures. Some of the greatest inventors have "failed their way to the top." Remember the Thomas Edison story. It's forging ahead and not being afraid to make a mistake. The mistake will come, don't worry about that. But allow that mistake to lead you in a new and better direction.

2. **Fear of Taking Risks** – Risk-taking oftentimes gets a bad rap. When we hear the word "risk" we automatically get into panic mode but this is also the reason why most of us are stuck. Getting unstuck requires a certain amount of risk taking. You must take some risks to achieve results. We take risks everyday although we don't recognize them as risks. When we drive to work you put yourself at risk of potentially getting into an accident. Will that stop you from driving? In my opinion, risks are recognizing the potential threat or possibility of danger but pressing on anyway in a calculated and cautious manner. Taking the risk doesn't always feel right or feel good. Get your feelings out of the way and just do it!

Another way to describe taking risks is to step out on faith or stepping into boldness. We talked about that one mustard seed of faith in the previous chapter and how that requires looking at the possibilities and not the limitations. When you take risks you are stepping out when your feelings are usually telling you to step back. Perhaps you've made up some reason/excuse why taking this risk is going to fail and result in embarrassment or humiliation. Let me qualify this statement by saying, there are times we should evaluate the situation, look at the facts and make an informed decision based on the facts. If sirens are going off in your head with big bright DANGER signs, consider a different move or approach. When you are able to identify that it's the fear of taking risks that's holding you back you can make a decision in that moment to evaluate the risk, tuck your feelings aside, and step out on faith.

3. **Fear of Greater Responsibility** – This is a biggie in the fear department. Another word for responsibility is ACCOUNTABILITY. It's one thing to be accountable to yourself but when you have to be accountable to somebody or for something, the fear increases. Look at the two examples. It was the thought of greater responsibility that prevented one individual from accepting a promotion. Do we see that often in the workplace? In business decisions? When something goes wrong, who's to blame?

Here's a thought, would we mind the greater responsibility if we knew nothing would ever go wrong and if it did, we wouldn't be blamed? If that's the case, then what we fear most is how we are viewed by other people and what people think about us. We enjoy the power but not the responsibility that comes along with it. "With great power comes great responsibility."

4. **Fear of Uncertainty and Doubt** – Have you ever felt insecure? Of course you have. Whether it was about your appearance or in your abilities, we've all felt it at some point. I'd even go as far as saying, that we're tested in the areas of insecurity, uncertainty and self-doubt daily. As confident and as assertive as I know that I am, I am surely tested in these areas. I tend to see it most as a new opportunity presents itself and I'm uncertain if I'm qualified. I also witness this type of uncertainty in my clients when we work on new behaviors or activities that are out of their "comfort zone." They begin to doubt their abilities.

This type of fear, in my opinion, can be overcome by one simple activity: Blockers and Builders exercise. Identify what's blocking your progress, imagined or real, (Blockers) and learn to combat the negative, false beliefs with "truths" (Builders). We tend to make up stuff and the more we make it up, the more we tend to believe it's true. You'll get a chance to do this exercise in the next chapter.

"Get your feelings out of the way and just do it!"

101 Excuses

Some of the most common excuses we've all heard that stem from FEAR.

Career – Excuses we make up why we don't pursue career aspirations or opportunities or stay in poor jobs.

1. I'm not qualified

2. I don't have a degree

3. What are my friends going to say

4. I'm too old

5. I don't have money to

6. I'm afraid of what I don't know

7. What if it doesn't work out

8. Things might get better here

9. I won't get this salary anywhere else

10. Who else is going to hire me in this economy

11. What else can I do?

12. My boss isn't really that bad

Relationships – Why we settle and stay in unsatisfactory relationships.

1. I'm too old look for somebody new

2. Familiarity

3. I'm comfortable

4. I don't want to be alone

5. I'm in love

6. I don't want to break up the family

7. I don't want to raise the kids alone

8. It will get better

9. He's/She's good enough for me

10. I'm financially secure

Healthy Lifestyle – Poor Health Choices and reasons why we don't exercise and live a healthy lifestyle which may be fear of failing in this area.

1. It's too hard to eat healthy

2. It's too difficult to lose weight

3. I don't have time

4. Healthy food is too expensive

5. I'm too tired

6. I don't know what to do

7. It's inconvenient

8. I'm not that overweight

9. It's boring

10. Healthy food is bland

Financial Freedom/Flexibility – Excuses people make about managing their money, investing and saving that may stem from FEAR.

1. Stock market is risky

2. Only the wealthy make money in investments

3. What if I lose all my money

4. I don't know where to begin

5. Managing money is too difficult

6. I seem to be managing just fine on my own

7. I need to make more money at my job, then I'll save more

8. I invested once before and lost money

9. My money is safer in a bank

10. My money is safer underneath my mattress

The purpose of this chapter is to help you recognize that fear is a huge factor when you reference defeat. Fear of failing, greater responsibility, taking risks and uncertainty. There are more types of fear such as fear of success which is a close relative of fear of greater responsibility. When we succeed, others expect more from us and we expect more from ourselves. And if we "fail" to live up to those expectations immediately, we can get discouraged and oftentimes display a "give-up" attitude which can drive some of the other fears.

Get clear on your fears and acknowledge them, don't run from them. The "builders and blockers" exercise will allow you to confront and combat."

Chapter takeaway: *What's one area in your life that is a challenge and may stem from FEAR?*

What type of fear is it and how will you begin to change?

Changing My Thoughts and Perceptions

Write down how your thoughts and perceptions on self-defeat have changed after reading this chapter.

CHAPTER 5

The Breakthrough

*"Keep your dreams alive. Understand to achieve anything requires faith
and belief in yourself, vision, hard work, determination, and dedication.
Remember all things are possible for those who believe."* —Gail Devers

For the past 4 years I have taken a kickboxing class. When I put on my gloves and hit that bag I feel so powerful, in control and free. I'm ready to take on any challenge that comes my way. It's a place where I feel the most alive, energized and confident. There is no judgment but support. There is no contempt for others but respect. There is no dissatisfaction but enjoyment. This has become a cathartic place for me when life's obstacles try to break me down. As a result, I get a "breakthrough" and not broken down. YES!

The more time I spend at my kickboxing class the more clear I am about my purpose. There's nothing like punching and kicking a bag to get clear on your purpose. When judgment comes, kick it to the curb. If contempt enters your space, knock it down. I know it sounds simple and it really is that simple once you value your life more and get out of the "defeated zone." It's important that you identify a safe place where you feel this free, in control and powerful. Allow it to gradually spill over in other areas in your life.

"Get a breakthrough and not broken down."

Have you ever experienced one amazing breakthrough? A breakthrough or ah-ha moment is a revelation of something so powerful that it may move you to tears or prompt you take immediate action. I had a breakthrough when someone once told me that there is a reason why the windshield of a car is larger than the rear view mirror. We need to spend more time looking forward than looking back. There comes a time when looking back and reflecting is necessary. We gain insight and discernment in past decisions and/or actions. Have you ever asked yourself, "How did I get here?" It's a powerful question that prompts you to think and maybe even admit that you have made some mistakes and poor decisions that led you here.

Another breakthrough came to me in these words, "We're letting you go." Not at all how I would have envisioned a breakthrough but there was a lesson to be learned. It turned out to be a lesson of **feeling powerless, not in control** and **restricted.**

"In this ring, we have…"

In 2009, I was expecting my 2nd child and working in a Director role at a financial institution. I was directly responsible for a team of Managers and oversaw the largest and most productive region in our sales division. This opportunity as an Director came about quickly. I was promoted 18 months after joining the company, received recognition for outstanding results and was now part of the Strategic Planning team headed up by the CEO and other Senior Executives. I was making more money than I had in past positions. I felt well respected among my peers and had tenure in the organization. Life was good…or was it?

The Sucker Punch

Shortly before I began my maternity leave I noticed a shift in our department. Things began to be more cutthroat and people were leaving, some voluntarily and some involuntarily. It created concern and I felt powerless and not at all in control because I wasn't. The day I was scheduled to take my maternity leave I receive a call stating that our division is changing and that I would no longer be needed as a Director but that I would remain in a different capacity when I returned from my leave. Shocking and disturbing news for a mother-to-be, 4 weeks away from giving birth. I was entering into the "defeated zone" feeling powerless and like a loser.

When I returned 4 months after giving birth, in my "new" demoted role, I had a breakthrough. "Why am I still here?" Title or no title. Job or no job. I was compromising my joy everyday working in that place. And when I got home to my husband and kids, my mood didn't change much. It was clear that it was affecting my life and the people around me. The day finally came where I had to make a decision about my future. As I started to look out of the windshield (metaphorically speaking) to my future, I saw a more confident and happier me. So, *I* mentally made the decision that I was ready to go!

Now, if you recall I stated earlier that I was "let go" from my job. So, you might be thinking, "well how did *you* make the decision to move one when they let you go?" I had already made it up in my mind that I was moving on. The small but significant detail was the sequence of events that led up to my departure. In specific terms, I wasn't exactly certain how it was going to happen. When we don't take charge of a situation, divine intervention will. It was a victorious win! I'm writing about it now in this published book as an Author, Speaker and CEO of my company, so I would deem that as a real victory!

"When we don't take charge of a situation, divine intervention will."

And the Winner Is…

Winning is not about a perceived victory based on money, status or friends. You are the victor when you come through a situation that feels unbeatable and you push passed it. Now, if I had stayed in a "defeated mind-set" and focused being let-go and looking out the rear view mirror, then I *would* have been defeated. I redirected my focus and committed myself to my future. I refused to allow that ONE circumstance to bring me down or cause me to doubt my abilities. So I was a WINNER! I came out more confident, in control, free and powerful! Oftentimes when we face unfortunate situations or something unexpected happens to us we immediately fall into a defeated mind-set. *Teaching moment.* We tend to focus on what is and not what could be. *The now and not the possibilities.* That's how we get stuck in fear, doubt, hopelessness, and worry. What I felt was a real and genuine concern. I didn't know what I would be doing. But

I didn't stay in that space. I pushed passed the "perceived defeat" and into the actual victory by focusing on my future possibilities.

"We tend to focus on what is and not what could be; the now and not the possibilities."

Rule #1

Don't get so caught up at the amusement park that you can't see the exit sign! The facts were I wasn't growing. I was unhappy and unfulfilled. Rule #1: If you really want to know what's keeping you stuck or in the "defeated zone", take this next exercise to help you with uncovering the answers. First, I want you to write down one goal that you have not yet achieved. Second, list 10 reasons that are limiting you from achieving this goal today?

Dream or Goal:

_____

_____

_____

_____

_____

Dream Blockers:

1.

2.

3.

4.

5.

6.

7.

8.

9.

10.

Did your response include items such as money, time, family, or spouse, basically anything that points outward away from you. I want you to revisit your answer and this time direct them inward, reflecting on you. I know you're thinking, "Why didn't you say that in the first place." There's a good reason for that. It's important that you answered naturally and candidly without any influence so that you can visually see your limiting beliefs. If you can learn something, you can unlearn something. This is a learning exercise how to change your mind-set and decipher the real reasons why you're stuck and perhaps feeling defeated.

Complete the exercise again. Take note how your answers change. Do they now include things like:

- Fear

- Worry

- Lack of determination

- Lack of commitment

- Behavior

- Attitude

- A plan or strategy

- Set goal

- Lack of focus

- Knowledge

- Required skills

Dream Blockers are defined as FEAR, limiting beliefs and they can:

- Inhibit personal growth

- Create a false perception of truth

- Prevents forward movement

- Stifles pursuing your passion

- Keep you down

"Don't get so caught up at the amusement park (yourself) that you can't see the exit sign!"

Dream Builders

If *Dream Blockers* are equivalent to an opponent or the enemy, then *Dream Builders* will be the armor. Dream Builders are internal attributes like drive, ambition, tenacity, passion, optimism, determination, and commitment. Through these intangibles you can obtain the tangibles. Write down 10 *Dream Builders* that will help you achieve one dream or goal today. I want you to select only ONE from your list that you can commit to today and begin focusing your energy in that direction. If it's ambition, then let that become a focal point in your plan and execution strategy. Allow that to become part of your daily lingo. Act as though you are what you claim to be. "Hello, my name is Tiana and I'm ambitious!" That one tweak in language, creates a change in your mind which fosters confidence and attracts people to you!

Dream Builders

1.

2.

3.

4.

5.

6.

7.

8.

9.

10.

Dreams Builders are defined as having drive, vision, commitment and they...

• Get you unstuck!

• Manifest hope and possibilities

• Spark creativity

• Maintain your focus and keep you on course

• Build you up!

I believe this chapter will be an "ah-ha" moment for you. Are you wrestling with making a decision about something you've been putting off for a long time? Are you tired of settling? Do you want your joy and peace back in your life? Get a "breakthrough" and not broken down! Spend time becoming clear about your purpose. Don't allow judgement or contempt to enter your space and never, EVER sacrifice your joy.

Chapter Takeaways: *What's one area in your life that you need to take charge over that is causing you to feel powerless, not in control and unfulfilled?*

Changing My Thoughts and Perceptions

Write down how your thoughts and perceptions on self-defeat have changed after reading this chapter.

CHAPTER 6

Out of the
Defeated
Zone and Into
Determination

"He who is not courageous enough to take risks
will accomplish nothing in life." —Muhammad Ali

Today, I had a conversation with a woman who recently started her own business. When I asked her how she was doing in the business she responded unenthusiastically, "it's ok." She went on to tell me that the business had not really taken off because she was stuck in FEAR. Fear of failure, fear of greater responsibility, fear of taking risks, or fear of uncertainty and doubt. Whatever type of fear she had, it was preventing her from moving forward. When you are stuck in fear you are giving permission for defeat to enter! *Teaching moment*

I remember vividly being in that same space and it wasn't that long ago. Starting a business isn't for everyone, if it were then everyone would be doing it! You experience rejection, failure and incredible challenges. You feel as though it can't possibly get any worse, and then it does. It can become the biggest test of your faith. Remember, it's not what happens to you that defines you but how you come out on the other side. You find out what you're really made of and how much you can handle. But there's one ingredient that separates the winners from the losers –DETERMINATION!

"When you are stuck in fear you are giving permission for defeat to enter!"

One Main Ingredient

If you recall in Chapter 3 , "the little something extra we need to achieve our goal (success) is **determination**, drive, ambition with a dash of perseverance." Without that main ingredient, you may end up in the "defeated zone." If you have ever baked a cake, you know that the recipe requires a specific set of ingredients. If one ingredient is off by even a fraction, it changes the texture, taste and consistency of the cake. One negative thought, wavering faith, doubt, uncertainty or fear will put you in the zone.

Signs of Being in and out of the Defeated Zone

A determined person has a strong mind and strong character. They may experience fear but they push through it. Fear without action is letting the "defeat" win. Fear is evident. Fear exists. The key is when you feel fear, don't run from it. Acknowledge it and do it anyway. That is "fear with action."

A determined person has a fixed purpose, will and intention. They are solution-oriented and action-oriented individuals. They are determined to succeed. Success is incremental and along with success comes failure. A determined person embraces failure as part of the process and remains focused. My belief is that achieving success and the difference between winning and losing should also be based on one's character. Look at some main characteristics of a determined person:

20 Characteristics of a Determined Person ·

1. Steps out on faith

2. Is bold and confident when facing any challenge or obstacle

3. Is not shaken by a temporary set-back or "perceived defeat."

4. Sees the roadblock ahead but finds a way around it.

5. Unrelenting when the going gets tough.

6. Able to push through rejection

7. Does not give into defeat

8. Lives by the slogan, "try and try again."

9. Takes risks and sees the possibilities and not the limitations

10. Self-motivated

11. Focused

12. Driven

13. Committed

14. Maintains a high-degree of energy

15. Not fearful of competition

16. Prepares for life's challenges

17. Resilient

18. Has unwavering FAITH

19. Believes in the possibilities

20. Has incredible perseverance!

Activities of a Determined Person

A determined person doesn't wait for things to fall into their lap. They go after it with a plan and purpose. They already deem themselves as winners so the activity is a formality, a necessary formality. A determined person reveals nothing. They act. They do. They don't spend time talking about what they're going to do, they just do it. Notice the activities of a determined person and see where you fit in

<u>Execute</u> – Determined people will get the job done. It may be swift or take some time but they are fixed on the purpose until they succeed.

<u>Evaluate</u> – A determined person assesses the situation to find the best course of action. They gauge the severity of the situation to make the best and most effective decision.

<u>Prioritize</u> – Determined people create a sense of urgency with tasks. They realize the importance of accomplishing the objective(s) and regard it as critical.

Produces – Determined people are producers. Again it may be swift or take time but they will achieve the goal. They understand that effort, activity and attitude are key contributors to achieving results.

Adjusts – A determined person can gauge when they need to adjust their efforts, activities and attitude to produce the best results. They don't wait for direction or guidance.

Plans – A determined person formulates plans to get the best results. They put together the best strategy and execute it. They may have multiple plans and strategies. They are prepared for the unexpected and able to change direction without hesitation.

Creates Meaningful Goals – A determined person uses the SMART goal setting process. They set **S**mart, **M**easurable, **A**chievable, **R**ealistic, and **T**ime-Bound goals. This becomes a measuring stick for achieving the goal and holding themselves accountable.

Creates Daily Objectives – A determined person outlines daily tasks to achieve the best results. No day is wasted. They mobilize their resources to get the most out of each day. They're not time wasters or time robbers.

As I mentioned in Chapter 5, regarding Builders and Blockers, there are many internal hindrances that could keep you stuck and prevent you from moving forward. The one characteristic I believe wholeheartedly that will get you unstuck and out of the "defeated zone" is pure **determination**.

Chapter Takeaways: *What's one characteristic of determination that you possess?*

Changing My Thoughts and Perceptions

Write down how your thoughts and perceptions on self-defeat have changed after reading this chapter.

CHAPTER 7

THE UNDEFEATED ONE

"Yet amid all these things, we are more than conquerors and gain a surpassing victory through Him Who loved us."
—Romans 8:37 Amplified Bible

Today is February 3, 2013. This day has new meaning for me. This day means hope, determination, and re-birth. I made a purposeful decision to write this chapter last and on this day. Today my sister celebrates her 40th birthday. This is a triumphant occasion because five weeks prior, I didn't know if she would make it to see this day. My sister's story has given me a new perspective on overcoming defeat and the power of faith. With her permission, I share this story to inspire, encourage and uplift.

Christmas 2012

December 13th, 2012 was a day I will never forget. I woke up ready for the day with a high degree of energy and positive attitude. I was preparing for a productive work day as business was picking up. Usually, I head to Starbucks for a latte to jump start my day. I'm in line of the local Starbucks when my phone rings. I recognize the number and answer the call. "Pull over," says the person on the other end. Not exactly the way I expected to be greeted. Again, "pull over," I hear repeated. Well, I was in the line at Starbucks and there really wasn't anyplace for me to go. I ease my way up to the window and "hush" the Barista as I listen to what's coming out on the other end of the phone.

I'm in a nearby parking lot, with a hot cup of coffee and motionless. I was just told that my sister, while getting a routine procedure, experienced a "complication." Her heart stopped. She went into cardiac arrest. Not once. Not twice. But three times. She was 39 years old. I listened as the doctor explained what happened, catching words and phrases only. Never did I imagine that my day would begin like this when I awoke that morning. I got off the phone and on the freeway, praying the whole way. Strength comes at the right moment.

Who Is This

I arrived to the hospital unafraid. That probably sounds crazy but I was remarkably calm and unafraid. I chose to look at the good which was that she is alive. Stable and alive. Although I didn't have the complete story yet, I was hopeful. My husband meets me in the lobby and we head to the ICU unit. While getting on the elevator I noticed this woman approaching. She gets inside the elevator and appears somewhat in a hurry. The elevator is getting a slow start moving so the woman decides to take the stairs instead. Not giving it a second thought we stay on the elevator and get to our destination. When we get off I see the same woman heading in the direction we were going. Again, not thinking too much about it we arrive at the double doors leading into the ICU unit. The double doors have windows which allowed us to see directly inside the ICU area. I try to get the attention of one of the nurses and doctors on the inside to let us in. But everyone appeared busy with other patients – one patient in particular. I found this odd and frustrating because directly in my line of sight were several doctors and nurses. They were gathered outside of the room near the entrance. The double doors are opening and closing as new people enter and exit. The third time the door opens I hear one of the doctors refer to that person in the room as a "she." I looked above the door at the room number and checked the slip of paper with my sister's room number, and it was the same.

Immediately, concern grew inside me. That calm, unafraid me was leaving. I began flailing my hands for attention and it worked. A doctor walks toward me as I tell him the person in that room is who we're here to see. As he's explaining, again catching words and phrases, the woman from the elevator appears. She heads directly to me and confusion sets in. "Who are you?" My first thought was that she was a doctor, a specialist perhaps. She hands me a card with her name on it and as I read it the word "Chaplin" stands out. What? A Chaplin is a priest, pastor and/or representative of the Christian Church. This changed everything. My sister's condition was obviously more serious than I realized. So much so that they deemed it necessary for a Chaplin to greet me.

The doctor is still speaking with my husband when the double doors open and I see my sister for the first time. She's on a gurney right in front of me and my face drops. Who is this? This is not my sister, but in fact it was. Her frail body, slightly opened eyes although it was clear she was unconscious, distorted mouth due to the tube hanging out of it and expressionless face. Me and my husband were the first to see her in this state after the cardiac arrest. Thank God he was with me. Thank God *HE* was with me too.

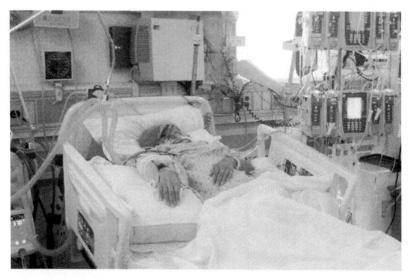

A Moment of Defeat

I'm a woman of faith able to overcome. Everything about me and what I stood for was going to be tested in the moments following the actual causes of her three cardiac arrests. Up until we arrived, information was given to us in waves. The first wave: my sister suffered a cardiac arrest. The second wave: she suffered a cardiac arrest due to plaque build-up in her artery which prevented the normal flow of blood to the heart. Third wave: she may have suffered brain damage from the lack of oxygen to her heart. Treacherous waves, I was wiped out. Confused and wiped out.

After hearing all of that, I was scared. Scared, afraid, anxious and any other worry-related word you can think of. I sat in the chair of the waiting room, put my hands over my face and started crying. I don't cry. I'm not an emotional creature that openly expresses her emotions especially in public. I excused myself to the bathroom to escape for a minute and collect my thoughts. I went into the nearest open stall, closed the door behind me and fell to my knees. I suffered an emotional breakdown right there in the bathroom. My knees buckled and I cried harder than I ever cried before.

The Odds Were Against Her

The trauma her heart suffered through the three cardiac arrests was concerning. Doctors were concerned that damage to the heart was irrevocable. They were also concerned that there could be damage to her brain. In the days to come, other areas in her body would become a concern: liver and kidneys. Again, she was 39 years old. To help her heart function, she was placed on a life support system. This life support system did the job her heart could not do. We were given a prognosis that the likelihood of the machine completing strengthening her heart was a 10-30% chance. This was on day one.

The Fight for Life

The fight for her life began the moment her heart stopped the first time. For a woman as young as she to have suffered a cardiac arrest, it was baffling to Doctors and nurses. The ICU unit can be a dreary place. Every patient is under critical care for a life threatening condition. To see a seemingly healthy, fit young woman in that place did not make sense. My brother captured all of our feelings after seeing her for the first time when he said, "Things do not make sense to me anymore." My sister was one of the youngest admitted at that time but her situation was by far the most baffling and concerning.

The first time I saw her in the ICU she had tube coming out of her mouth, breathing machine near her bed and an IV pole filled with bags all supplying various forms of medication. She didn't move. She didn't speak. She didn't open her eyes. She was heavily sedated. The first time they took her off sedation was to test her responsiveness. I remember standing nearby as the doctors woke her up. As she was waking up I remember thinking, she did suffer brain damage. Oh my God! She was infant-like and resembled characteristics of a mentally challenged person. I was terrified. Things did not make sense to *me* anymore. Each time they took her out of sedation, she displayed these infant-like signs but it lessened as the days went on. An MRI was needed to determine if her brain suffered any real damage. Make no mistake, she was fighting for her life.

The Opponent and My Test of Faith

Failed heart. Brain damage. Death. Her heart needed to fully recover on its own or she would need a heart transplant. Again I say, 39 years old. A heart transplant comes with its own set of risks not to mention locating a heart. This was a concept that I just could not wrap my head around. All of these thoughts and questions started to enter my mind. How soon can they locate a heart? What are the risks with this type of surgery? What happens if her body rejects the heart? Could the outcome be much worse? The same questions plagued my thoughts regarding the MRI. What quality of life will she have if the results come back unfavorable? I never uttered these concerns aloud but they were a concern. I was displaying signs of a defeated mind-set.

My faith was being tested. My faith in God, the doctors, nurses and her will to recover. One mustard seed of faith was all I needed. One positive thought to combat the negative thoughts in my head.

The Secret Weapon

You can't go into a fight ill-prepared. Before the fight you choose your weapons, armor and strategy. You research your opponent to develop your strategy and plan your successful win. This was an unfair fight in my opinion because my sister didn't have time to prepare and "gear up" for the fight. As unfair as it was, she showed up with heavy artillery. *The Doctors.* The Doctors were highly effective and helped in conquering the medical challenges. Doctors, doctors and more doctors! She had a nurse assigned solely to her 24 hours a day due to her critical state. There was never a time when I visited, that a nurse or doctor was not present. *The Support.* The support of family and friends provided the positive ammunition needed to overcome doubt and create an encouraging atmosphere. *Faith.* Faith in her FULL recovery was one of the biggest weapons we had in this fight. *Determination.* My sister was determined to live. Period.

Through and Through

Day 1 rolled into day 2. Day 5 turned into day 7. Day 7 soon became day 13. Every day was a different day. Every day brought new challenges and new triumphs. Days starting blending together and I couldn't tell one day from the next. Phone calls and text messages consumed half of my day as I updated close family and friends on her progress. New doctors, old nurses, new nurses and old doctors. MRI test – good. No known damage. Liver and kidneys improved.

Her heart began to recover and function on its own. This was a huge hurdle in the process of her recovery. I wrote in a journal throughout this experience and I recall writing this on day 7:

> *What I remember most about today is it's a BIG DAY! No more life support machine! Your scheduled surgery is today; Dr. Ramzy is optimistic; you are never awake when I visit; do you know I've been here every day? The days are jumbled together – no sense of time. Mom is a trooper! Waiting, thinking, praying and waiting for the surgery to be over. Back to where it all began in this waiting room. The news is great! We are grateful. No more machine! No more hole! Best day yet!*

The hole I'm referring to is a hole in her heart. More tests showed that a blood clot developed and entered her heart through a hole. The doctors were able to repair the hole. No hole meant no more heart transplant. The following day, day 8 I wrote this:

> *What I remember most about today is you speaking. You told me to sit down and get some coffee. Your voice is a whisper but audible and clear. You're in pain. Your feet hurt. You asking question after question. I remember you saying, "trust yourself. I'm fighting for my life. I'm scared. I love you." I remember your sense of humor while I rubbed your feet and you telling me "keep jiggling Peggy."*

"Keep jiggling Peggy" was a line from one of my favorite TV shows, I Love Lucy. My sister was referring to the pain in her legs and feet and to keep rubbing them (jiggling). That funny, insignificant line was indeed very significant to me. She was speaking. She was alert. She was cracking jokes. My sister was back.

On Day 11, I wrote:

What I remember most about today is that it's almost Christmas. You've been here almost two weeks. You're hungry and thirsty. You got out of the bed and into the chair and that made you happy. Your breathing is much better. You liked therapy today. We watched a holiday movie, The Polar Express. That made you happy. Brother bought your favorite holiday CD, Andrea Bocelli. You're getting more feisty – that's good! You're smiling today – that's good! The word of the day is "PROGRESS!"

The day she left ICU, day 14, I wrote:

What I remember most about today is no more ICU! Thank you Jesus! You have a new room. You look so much better. We spent the evening watching movies and talking. You begin to understand what happened to you and why you were in the ICU. I give you information in doses to gauge your reaction. You're taking the news unbelievable well. I don't think it has sunk in. I mention to you that you should journal about this experience. You came up with a title, "There and back again…"

The Victory

28 days was the total number of days my sister was in the hospital. It's a true miracle. The doctors and nurses are still in disbelief of her

overall recovery. Every day, while in the hospital, doctors and nurses would enter her room and comment, "Wow! You look so much better!" This would always take my sister by surprise because she had little knowledge of her entire ordeal only what she heard from staff and family. The day she left the hospital we were overjoyed. She overcame a huge feat and is a victor not a victim! Her experience reminds me how strong we all are and how much we can endure. We are resilient, determined fighters that when our internal drive is activated, there is nothing we cannot overcome.

The Revelation

I am grateful for this experience as it has revealed many things to me. Odds were against my sister due to the trauma her heart suffered. We chose, as a family, not be deterred by the news and percentages but focus on the positive outcome – the possibilities and not the limitations. When the news came through about the hole in her heart and possible damage to the brain, we spoke words of life and believed in a full recovery. Every word spoke was acting as though she were already fully healed. Words are powerful. Our family and friends rallied with us, faith-filled and determined to see a complete recovery. It was difficult at times to see the positive outcome but defeat was never an option. Every small improvement in her condition, we celebrated. She opened her eyes, we celebrated. Her heart slowly began to function on its own, we celebrated. She sat up in a chair, we celebrated. She walked, we celebrated. We didn't wait until she was out of the hospital before we celebrated in her achievements. And today, we celebrate as she turns 40 and is here, fully recovered and re-born. She fought the good fight and came out victorious (winner) on the other side.

Changing My Thoughts and Perceptions

Write down how your thoughts and perceptions on self-defeat have changed after reading this chapter.

CHAPTER 8

3 1 PRINCIPLES
OF CONQUERING
DEFEAT

"One Principle a day keeps the defeat away!" —Tiana Sanchez

Becoming undefeatable is about picking yourself up when you are faced with difficult challenges. It's about overcoming those temporary set-backs and not allowing the "now" to define you. It's about determination, the true measurement of success. Remember, a determined person sees the roadblocks ahead but finds a way around it. Winning and losing is not about how much money you have, how much you can prove by attaining "material" success but by your ability to press on – your determined character.

This chapter is designed to guide you in becoming UNDEFEATABLE in areas in your life, career, business and health. It is ultimately designed for your personal and professional development. These 31 principles are the KEY teachable moments, lessons, tips, and strategies learned in this book. I selected 5 principles from each chapter to help you create a daily lesson plan and get you out of DEFEAT. Read each principle and see how it applies in your life. Identify blockers that are keeping you in the "defeated zone." Ask yourself questions about challenges you are experiencing right now and how it's impacting your ability to move forward. Are you stuck? Are you afraid? What type of fear is holding you back? Write a commitment to yourself on the effort, activity and attitude you need to "win" in that area.

Whether you are an entrepreneur, athlete, teacher, CEO, student, Coach or professional. We all have felt a sense of defeat in our lives and I'm here to tell you that you may fail, heck you may fail several times but what you will not be is DEFEATED!

Day 1 Principle:

Change Your Perception- *Perceived Defeat is not Defeat*

What is ONE shift you can make today to become UNDEFEATABLE in this area?

Identify the "Blockers" that could put you in the "defeated zone" today? *(list in "Blockers" column)*

What do you <u>have</u> already that will help you WIN in this area? (List in *"Builders" column*)

Builders   # Blockers

- ☐ Ambition   ☐ Doubt
- ☐ Optimism   ☐ Uncertainty
- ☐ Determination   ☐ Fear
- ☐   ☐
- ☐   ☐

Daily Commitment to Yourself:
Effort (I will put forth), Activity (I will do), Attitude (I will have)

Day 2 Principle:

Character – *True Measurement of Winning and Losing*

What is ONE shift you can make today to become UNDEFEATABLE in this area?

Identify the "Blockers" that could put you in the "defeated zone" today? *(list in "Blockers" column)*

What do you <u>have</u> already that will help you WIN in this area? (List in *"Builders" column*)

Builders

- [ ] Ambition
- [ ] Optimism
- [ ] Determination
- [ ]
- [ ]

Blockers

- [ ] Doubt
- [ ] Uncertainty
- [ ] Fear
- [ ]
- [ ]

Daily Commitment to Yourself:

Effort (I will put forth), Activity (I will do), Attitude (I will have)

Day 3 Principle:

Results - *Effort + Activity + Attitude = WIN!*

What is ONE shift you can make today to become UNDEFEATABLE in this area?

Identify the "Blockers" that could put you in the "defeated zone" today? *(list in "Blockers" column)*

What do you <u>have</u> already that will help you WIN in this area? (List in *"Builders" column*)

Builders

Blockers

☐ Ambition	☐ Doubt
☐ Optimism	☐ Uncertainty
☐ Determination	☐ Fear
☐	☐
☐	☐

Daily Commitment to Yourself:

Effort (I will put forth), Activity (I will do), Attitude (I will have)

Day 4 Principle:

Ambition and Drive – *Activate Your Internal Drive*

What is ONE shift you can make today to become UNDEFEATABLE in this area?

Identify the "Blockers" that could put you in the "defeated zone" today? *(list in "Blockers" column)*

What do you <u>have</u> already that will help you WIN in this area? (List in *"Builders" column*)

Builders   # Blockers

Builders	Blockers
☐ Ambition	☐ Doubt
☐ Optimism	☐ Uncertainty
☐ Determination	☐ Fear
☐	☐
☐	☐

Daily Commitment to Yourself:

Effort (I will put forth), Activity (I will do), Attitude (I will have)

Day 5 Principle:

Mind-Set – *A Defeated Mind is Toxic*

What is ONE shift you can make today to become UNDEFEATABLE in this area?

Identify the "Blockers" that could put you in the "defeated zone" today? *(list in "Blockers" column)*

What do you <u>have</u> already that will help you WIN in this area? (List in *"Builders" column*)

Builders   # Blockers

Builders	Blockers
☐ Ambition	☐ Doubt
☐ Optimism	☐ Uncertainty
☐ Determination	☐ Fear
☐	☐
☐	☐

Daily Commitment to Yourself:
Effort (I will put forth), Activity (I will do), Attitude (I will have)

Day 6 Principle:

One Degree - *Make a Slight Change and Produce BIG Results*

What is ONE shift you can make today to become UNDEFEATABLE in this area?

Identify the "Blockers" that could put you in the "defeated zone" today? *(list in "Blockers" column)*

What do you <u>have</u> already that will help you WIN in this area? (List in *"Builders" column*)

Builders	Blockers
☐ Ambition	☐ Doubt
☐ Optimism	☐ Uncertainty
☐ Determination	☐ Fear
☐	☐
☐	☐

Daily Commitment to Yourself:

Effort (I will put forth), Activity (I will do), Attitude (I will have)

<u>Day 7 Principle</u>:

Visualize - *Look Out of the Windshield and not the Rearview Mirror*

What is ONE shift you can make today to become UNDEFEATABLE in this area?

Identify the "Blockers" that could put you in the "defeated zone" today? *(list in "Blockers" column)*

What do you <u>have</u> already that will help you WIN in this area? (List in *"Builders" column*)

Builders

Blockers

Builders	Blockers
☐ Ambition	☐ Doubt
☐ Optimism	☐ Uncertainty
☐ Determination	☐ Fear
☐	☐
☐	☐

Daily Commitment to Yourself:

Effort (I will put forth), Activity (I will do), Attitude (I will have)

Day 8 Principle:

Faith – *All You Need is One Mustard Seed of Faith*

What is ONE shift you can make today to become UNDEFEATABLE in this area?

Identify the "Blockers" that could put you in the "defeated zone" today? *(list in "Blockers" column)*

What do you <u>have</u> already that will help you WIN in this area? (List in *"Builders" column*)

Builders   # Blockers

☐ Ambition   ☐ Doubt

☐ Optimism   ☐ Uncertainty

☐ Determination   ☐ Fear

☐   ☐

☐   ☐

Daily Commitment to Yourself:

Effort (I will put forth), Activity (I will do), Attitude (I will have)

Day 9 Principle:

Celebrate – *Enjoy Every Small Achievement*

What is ONE shift you can make today to become UNDEFEATABLE in this area?

Identify the "Blockers" that could put you in the "defeated zone" today? *(list in "Blockers" column)*

What do you <u>have</u> already that will help you WIN in this area? (List in *"Builders" column*)

Builders   Blockers

☐ Ambition   ☐ Doubt

☐ Optimism   ☐ Uncertainty

☐ Determination   ☐ Fear

☐   ☐

☐   ☐

Daily Commitment to Yourself:

Effort (I will put forth), Activity (I will do), Attitude (I will have)

<u>Day 10 Principle</u>:

Determination – *The One Main Ingredient You Can't Do Without*
What is ONE shift you can make today to become UNDEFEATABLE in this area?

Identify the "Blockers" that could put you in the "defeated zone" today? *(list in "Blockers" column)*
What do you <u>have</u> already that will help you WIN in this area? (List in *"Builders" column*)

Builders   # Blockers

☐ Ambition   ☐ Doubt

☐ Optimism   ☐ Uncertainty

☐ Determination   ☐ Fear

☐   ☐

☐   ☐

Daily Commitment to Yourself:
Effort (I will put forth), Activity (I will do), Attitude (I will have)

Day 11 Principle:

Success – *It's not a One-Time Event*

What is ONE shift you can make today to become UNDEFEATABLE in this area?

Identify the "Blockers" that could put you in the "defeated zone" today? *(list in "Blockers" column)*

What do you <u>have</u> already that will help you WIN in this area? (List in *"Builders" column*)

Builders   # Blockers

☐ Ambition   ☐ Doubt

☐ Optimism   ☐ Uncertainty

☐ Determination   ☐ Fear

☐   ☐

☐   ☐

Daily Commitment to Yourself:

Effort (I will put forth), Activity (I will do), Attitude (I will have)

Day 12 Principle:

Powerful Words – *If You Say You Can't, Then You Won't*

What is ONE shift you can make today to become UNDEFEATABLE in this area?

Identify the "Blockers" that could put you in the "defeated zone" today? *(list in "Blockers" column)*

What do you <u>have</u> already that will help you WIN in this area? (List in *"Builders" column*)

Builders   # Blockers

☐ Ambition   ☐ Doubt

☐ Optimism   ☐ Uncertainty

☐ Determination   ☐ Fear

☐   ☐

☐   ☐

Daily Commitment to Yourself:
Effort (I will put forth), Activity (I will do), Attitude (I will have)

Day 13 Principle:

Fear – *Fear is Evident, So Do it Afraid*

What is ONE shift you can make today to become UNDEFEATABLE in this area?

Identify the "Blockers" that could put you in the "defeated zone" today? *(list in "Blockers" column)*

What do you <u>have</u> already that will help you WIN in this area? (List in *"Builders" column*)

Builders   # Blockers

☐ Ambition   ☐ Doubt

☐ Optimism   ☐ Uncertainty

☐ Determination   ☐ Fear

☐   ☐

☐   ☐

Daily Commitment to Yourself:

Effort (I will put forth), Activity (I will do), Attitude (I will have)

Day 14 Principle:

Mistakes Are OK – *Mistakes Lead you in a Better Direction*

What is ONE shift you can make today to become UNDEFEATABLE in this area?

Identify the "Blockers" that could put you in the "defeated zone" today? *(list in "Blockers" column)*

What do you <u>have</u> already that will help you WIN in this area? (List in *"Builders" column*)

Builders   # Blockers

☐ Ambition		☐ Doubt
☐ Optimism		☐ Uncertainty
☐ Determination		☐ Fear
☐		☐
☐		☐

Daily Commitment to Yourself:

Effort (I will put forth), Activity (I will do), Attitude (I will have)

Day 15 Principle:

Feelings – *Get Your Feelings Out of the Way and Just Do It*

What is ONE shift you can make today to become UNDEFEATABLE in this area?

Identify the "Blockers" that could put you in the "defeated zone" today? *(list in "Blockers" column)*

What do you have already that will help you WIN in this area? (List in *"Builders" column*)

Builders   Blockers

Builders	Blockers
☐ Ambition	☐ Doubt
☐ Optimism	☐ Uncertainty
☐ Determination	☐ Fear
☐	☐
☐	☐

Daily Commitment to Yourself:

Effort (I will put forth), Activity (I will do), Attitude (I will have)

Day 16 Principle:

Focus – *Get Clear on the Desired Results*

What is ONE shift you can make today to become UNDEFEATABLE in this area?

Identify the "Blockers" that could put you in the "defeated zone" today? *(list in "Blockers" column)*

What do you <u>have</u> already that will help you WIN in this area? (List in *"Builders" column*)

Builders	Blockers
☐ Ambition	☐ Doubt
☐ Optimism	☐ Uncertainty
☐ Determination	☐ Fear
☐	☐
☐	☐

Daily Commitment to Yourself:

Effort (I will put forth), Activity (I will do), Attitude (I will have)

Day 17 Principle:

Get a Revelation – *Revelations Can Be a Blessing*

What is ONE shift you can make today to become UNDEFEATABLE in this area?

Identify the "Blockers" that could put you in the "defeated zone" today? *(list in "Blockers" column)*

What do you <u>have</u> already that will help you WIN in this area? (List in *"Builders" column*)

Builders | # Blockers

Builders	Blockers
☐ Ambition	☐ Doubt
☐ Optimism	☐ Uncertainty
☐ Determination	☐ Fear
☐	☐
☐	☐

Daily Commitment to Yourself:

Effort (I will put forth), Activity (I will do), Attitude (I will have)

Day 18 Principle:

Get a Breakthrough – *Powerful, Free and In Control*

What is ONE shift you can make today to become UNDEFEATABLE in this area?

Identify the "Blockers" that could put you in the "defeated zone" today? *(list in "Blockers" column)*

What do you <u>have</u> already that will help you WIN in this area? (List in *"Builders" column*)

Builders	Blockers
☐ Ambition	☐ Doubt
☐ Optimism	☐ Uncertainty
☐ Determination	☐ Fear
☐	☐
☐	☐

Daily Commitment to Yourself:

Effort (I will put forth), Activity (I will do), Attitude (I will have)

Day 19 Principle:

Confidence – *Characteristic of a Determined Person*

What is ONE shift you can make today to become UNDEFEATABLE in this area?

Identify the "Blockers" that could put you in the "defeated zone" today? *(list in "Blockers" column)*

What do you <u>have</u> already that will help you WIN in this area? (List in *"Builders" column*)

Builders   Blockers

Builders	Blockers
☐ Ambition	☐ Doubt
☐ Optimism	☐ Uncertainty
☐ Determination	☐ Fear
☐	☐
☐	☐

Daily Commitment to Yourself:
Effort (I will put forth), Activity (I will do), Attitude (I will have)

Day 20 Principle:

Never Give Up - *Try and Try Again*

What is ONE shift you can make today to become UNDEFEATABLE in this area?

Identify the "Blockers" that could put you in the "defeated zone" today? *(list in "Blockers" column)*

What do you <u>have</u> already that will help you WIN in this area? (List in *"Builders" column*)

Builders   # Blockers

Builders	Blockers
☐ Ambition	☐ Doubt
☐ Optimism	☐ Uncertainty
☐ Determination	☐ Fear
☐	☐
☐	☐

Daily Commitment to Yourself:

Effort (I will put forth), Activity (I will do), Attitude (I will have)

Day 21 Principle:

Change Your Truth – *Truth or Something Made Up*

What is ONE shift you can make today to become UNDEFEATABLE in this area?

Identify the "Blockers" that could put you in the "defeated zone" today? *(list in "Blockers" column)*

What do you have already that will help you WIN in this area? (List in *"Builders" column*)

Builders	Blockers
☐ Ambition	☐ Doubt
☐ Optimism	☐ Uncertainty
☐ Determination	☐ Fear
☐	☐
☐	☐

Daily Commitment to Yourself:

Effort (I will put forth), Activity (I will do), Attitude (I will have)

Day 22 Principle:

Perseverance – *Purpose and Persistence*

What is ONE shift you can make today to become UNDEFEATABLE in this area?

Identify the "Blockers" that could put you in the "defeated zone" today? *(list in "Blockers" column)*

What do you <u>have</u> already that will help you WIN in this area? (List in *"Builders" column*)

Builders	Blockers
☐ Ambition	☐ Doubt
☐ Optimism	☐ Uncertainty
☐ Determination	☐ Fear
☐	☐
☐	☐

Daily Commitment to Yourself:

Effort (I will put forth), Activity (I will do), Attitude (I will have)

<u>Day 23 Principle</u>:

Prepare for the Fight – *Stay Ready*

What is ONE shift you can make today to become UNDEFEATABLE in this area?

Identify the "Blockers" that could put you in the "defeated zone" today? *(list in "Blockers" column)*

What do you <u>have</u> already that will help you WIN in this area? (List in *"Builders" column*)

Builders   # Blockers

☐ Ambition   ☐ Doubt

☐ Optimism   ☐ Uncertainty

☐ Determination   ☐ Fear

☐   ☐

☐   ☐

Daily Commitment to Yourself:
Effort (I will put forth), Activity (I will do), Attitude (I will have)

Day 24 Principle:

Know Your "Opponent" – *Build a Strategy to Defeat Your Opponent*
What is ONE shift you can make today to become UNDEFEATABLE in this area?

Identify the "Blockers" that could put you in the "defeated zone" today? *(list in "Blockers" column)*
What do you <u>have</u> already that will help you WIN in this area? (List in *"Builders" column*)

Builders   # Blockers

☐ Ambition   ☐ Doubt

☐ Optimism   ☐ Uncertainty

☐ Determination   ☐ Fear

☐   ☐

☐   ☐

Daily Commitment to Yourself:
Effort (I will put forth), Activity (I will do), Attitude (I will have)

Day 25 Principle:

Choose Your Amor – *Gear Up with Positive Artillery*

What is ONE shift you can make today to become UNDEFEATABLE in this area?

Identify the "Blockers" that could put you in the "defeated zone" today? *(list in "Blockers" column)*

What do you <u>have</u> already that will help you WIN in this area? (List in *"Builders" column*)

Builders   # Blockers

Builders	Blockers
☐ Ambition	☐ Doubt
☐ Optimism	☐ Uncertainty
☐ Determination	☐ Fear
☐	☐
☐	☐

Daily Commitment to Yourself:
Effort (I will put forth), Activity (I will do), Attitude (I will have)

Day 26 Principle:

Be Grateful – *Every Experience Has a Purpose*

What is ONE shift you can make today to become UNDEFEATABLE in this area?

Identify the "Blockers" that could put you in the "defeated zone" today? *(list in "Blockers" column)*

What do you <u>have</u> already that will help you WIN in this area? (List in *"Builders" column*)

Builders	Blockers
☐ Ambition	☐ Doubt
☐ Optimism	☐ Uncertainty
☐ Determination	☐ Fear
☐	☐
☐	☐

Daily Commitment to Yourself:

Effort (I will put forth), Activity (I will do), Attitude (I will have)

Day 27 Principle:

The Winning Truth – *Where Character Meets Determination*

What is ONE shift you can make today to become UNDEFEATABLE in this area?

Identify the "Blockers" that could put you in the "defeated zone" today? *(list in "Blockers" column)*

What do you <u>have</u> already that will help you WIN in this area? (List in *"Builders" column*)

Builders   # Blockers

☐ Ambition   ☐ Doubt

☐ Optimism   ☐ Uncertainty

☐ Determination   ☐ Fear

☐   ☐

☐   ☐

Daily Commitment to Yourself:
Effort (I will put forth), Activity (I will do), Attitude (I will have)

Day 28 Principle:

The Losing Truth – *You May Fail but You will Not be Defeated*

What is ONE shift you can make today to become UNDEFEATABLE in this area?

Identify the "Blockers" that could put you in the "defeated zone" today? *(list in "Blockers" column)*

What do you <u>have</u> already that will help you WIN in this area? (List in *"Builders" column*)

Builders	Blockers
☐ Ambition	☐ Doubt
☐ Optimism	☐ Uncertainty
☐ Determination	☐ Fear
☐	☐
☐	☐

Daily Commitment to Yourself:
Effort (I will put forth), Activity (I will do), Attitude (I will have)

Day 29 Principle:

Progress – *Keep an Internal Score of Your Progress*

What is ONE shift you can make today to become UNDEFEATABLE in this area?

Identify the "Blockers" that could put you in the "defeated zone" today? *(list in "Blockers" column)*

What do you <u>have</u> already that will help you WIN in this area? (List in *"Builders" column*)

Builders	Blockers
☐ Ambition	☐ Doubt
☐ Optimism	☐ Uncertainty
☐ Determination	☐ Fear
☐	☐
☐	☐

Daily Commitment to Yourself:
Effort (I will put forth), Activity (I will do), Attitude (I will have)

Day 30 Principle:

Affirm Your Undefeat – *You Are More Than a Conqueror*

What is ONE shift you can make today to become UNDEFEATABLE in this area?

Identify the "Blockers" that could put you in the "defeated zone" today? *(list in "Blockers" column)*

What do you <u>have</u> already that will help you WIN in this area? (List in *"Builders" column*)

Builders	Blockers
☐ Ambition	☐ Doubt
☐ Optimism	☐ Uncertainty
☐ Determination	☐ Fear
☐	☐
☐	☐

Daily Commitment to Yourself:

Effort (I will put forth), Activity (I will do), Attitude (I will have)

Day 31 Principle:

Claim The Victory – *Know That You've Won From the Start*

What is ONE shift you can make today to become UNDEFEATABLE in this area?

Identify the "Blockers" that could put you in the "defeated zone" today? *(list in "Blockers" column)*

What do you <u>have</u> already that will help you WIN in this area? (List in *"Builders" column*)

Builders   # Blockers

Builders	Blockers
☐ Ambition	☐ Doubt
☐ Optimism	☐ Uncertainty
☐ Determination	☐ Fear
☐	☐
☐	☐

Daily Commitment to Yourself:
Effort (I will put forth), Activity (I will do), Attitude (I will have)

MORE ABOUT THE AUTHOR

Tiana Sanchez grew up in Los Angeles, California and was the second child to her parents who advocated for issues surrounding equality and the rights of others. Her father, a bi-racial Mexican and African American and mother, African American. Growing up Tiana and her siblings faced many challenges. Not having enough money was a common theme in the household however they were never without anything. A faith-filled foundation was set early in Tiana's life through attending Church and reinforcing beliefs in the home. The biggest change occurred during the divorce of her parents on her 12th birthday. The divorce brought on new challenges and Tiana found herself shuffling from a shelter to a motel with her siblings.

At age 16 Tiana started working and was managing by 17. By age 22, Tiana was married with her first child. The marriage brought on new challenges and the relationship became a toxic one. Shortly after her son's first birthday, Tiana left the marriage and eventually divorced her husband. For several years, Tiana was a single Mother, working full time to support herself and her son. In 2001, two years after her divorce she met the man that would later become her husband.

Working full-time as a single mother, Tiana realized she needed a better plan for her future. She developed a 5-year plan with systems and processes that would later prove to be instrumental in designing the methodology in her coaching programs. Forging ahead through the downfall of the financial industry in 2008 and the continuous economic decline, Tiana persevered with determination and drive.

This internal drive led Tiana into a 15 year career in Management leading teams, training the best employees and ultimately launching her own coaching practice. She is currently Founder/Owner of **Tiana Sanchez Professional Coaching Services,** a company designed for personal and professional development by employing proven strategies and techniques to get her clients "unstuck." Tiana considers herself an "Empowering Agent." She has a proven record of providing clients the tools and easy-to-follow techniques that drive them to action! As a Business Owner and Coach, Tiana specializes in assisting men, women and youth in a non-threatening environment to *assess* their full potential, *coach* them forward, *execute* solution-based strategies and *follow up* with a self-correction process. With over 15 years of first-hand experience in personal and professional development, she is committed to results. Her customized approach aligns "real-life" experience and the "ideal life" desired from the client to transform strategies into action plans for success. This solution-based coaching style provides the client accountability, motivation and allows the client to access their internal resources to break through obstacles.

Tiana understands the importance of having a defined roadmap to achieve any level of success, undoubtedly learned from her childhood and work ethic.

Tiana currently lives in Los Angeles, California with her husband William and two boys, Tian age 14 and Salim age 3.

Company Overview and Scope of Services

Driven by the desire to help others become the catalyst for their future and with over 15 years of experience, Tiana Sanchez has developed a system that was created through weaving in the most effective development techniques and first-hand experience. This unique four-step system outlines behaviors and techniques that act as a "compass" to seamlessly guide the individual through the entire coaching process.

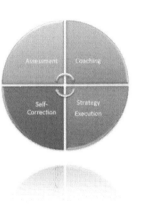

This system helps to assess a client's full potential, coach them forward, teach them how to execute strategies and then follow up with a self-correction process. Clients become accountable and stay fueled with motivation! Coaching is available in the following three areas for valued clients: Methods of Delivery: Onsite Presentation, One-on-One Coaching, Group Training, Webinar, and 2-4 Hour Workshops.

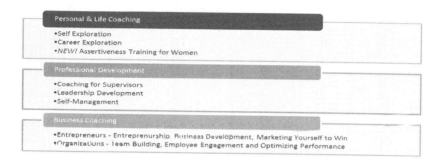

Personal & Life Coaching
- Self Exploration
- Career Exploration
- *NEW!* Assertiveness Training for Women

Professional Development
- Coaching for Supervisors
- Leadership Development
- Self-Management

Business Coaching
- Entrepreneurs - Entreprenurship, Business Development, Marketing Yourself to Win
- Organizations - Team Building, Employee Engagement and Optimizing Performance

Personal & Life Coaching

Self-Exploration

Identify your strengths and developmental opportunities, define your needs, access your internal resources and be your "own catalyst for change." Topics and Benefits may include:

➤ Ignite the Passion Within: Be Your Own Catalyst for Change

➤ Self-Exploration: 4 Stages – Explorer, Reflector, Forward Thinker, Driver

➤ Self-Awareness: Understanding Your Unique Personality Type

Career Exploration

Before you explore new career opportunities or leap into a new business relationship, it's imperative that you explore career interests and desires followed by exploring your professional interests. Topics and Benefits may include:

➤ Launching a Career Strategy: Career Planning, Assessment, and 7 Tips to Interviewing

➢ Developing a Post-College Strategy for Students

➢ Marketing Yourself to Win for Professionals, Students and Entrepreneurs

Assertiveness Training for Women

Are you willing to alter your behavior to develop a positive mind-set, a confident attitude, and portray a self-image that reflects your inner beauty and spirit? Topics may include:

➢ Eliminate Self-Destructive Behaviors that Inhibit Growth.

➢ Renew with Self-Affirming Behaviors to Gain Confidence

➢ Learn the how to Arm yourself with the ABC's of Assertiveness in your personal life and in the workplace: Assertiveness, Boldness, and Confidence.

Professional Leadership Development

Coaching for Supervisors

Equip the Management Team with effective tools and set and expectations from the beginning. Learn how to attack issues head-on, resolve conflict effectively and maintain the integrity of the company and individual through effective disciplinary techniques. Topics may include:

➢ The Art of Management

➢ The 10 Do's and Don'ts Every Supervisor Should Know

➢ It's Not Personal, It's Business: Balancing Empathy and Authority

Leadership Development

Have you ever wondered if you are an effective Leader or Manager Do you prefer to Manage processes or lead people? You have an enormous responsibility to coach and develop others, praise and build self-esteem, provide accountability, mentor, teach and inspire! Benefits and Topics may include:

➢ Influential Leadership: Learn the 7 areas that may directly affect your style of leadership

➢ Leadership Identification: Identify your unique Leadership style

➢ Self-Awareness and Self-Management

  ○ Self-Management - In order to be an effective individual, employee, or Supervisor you must understand how to manage your emotions and avoid a negative "emotional hijack." Emotional Intelligent Leaders have identified Self-Management as a leaders "primal challenge." Therefore managing ones emotions becomes vitally important to growth and development of the leader.

Business Coaching for Entrepreneurs

Entrepreneurship

Get an overview into the world on Entrepreneurship and craft your next big IDEA! "Strategic" Coaching Sessions (60 minutes) designed to help you monetize your DREAMS!

➢ Introduction to the World of Entrepreneurship and Crafting Your Next BIG IDEA

➢ From Baby Steps to Big Dreams: 7 ½ Steps to Realizing Your Passion & Monetizing Your Dreams

Business Development Plan

This is an Introduction to Starting Your Own Business. Learn the 9 Business Plan Essentials that provide a foundation and "roadmap" for successful operation of your business. Work through real-life exercises and experiences that will propel your business forward.

➢ Learn the 9 Business Plan Essentials

➢ The Power of Blogging and Becoming an Authority in Your Industry

Marketing Yourself to WIN! – Offered in a Webinar or group coaching only

Can you articulate who you are what you do and the value you bring in 30 seconds? There is a value equation that every entrepreneur and business professional should adopt. Get clear on your message and I will teach you how to become "sought after and not looked over."

➢ Leveraging Your Talents and Skills in Your Industry, Become a "Master" Connector, Create your "Pitch Kit" including a 30 Second Pitch, Expand Your Network Using Online and In-Person Social Platforms, Increasing Your Opportunities through Developing Strategic Alliances, Selecting a Coach or Mentor That's Right for You

Hear What Professionals & Business Owners are saying!

"Tiana Sanchez is a leading visionary in the field of career and management development. She transform's her client's lives by uncovering their greatest dreams and aspirations relating to their professional goals. She is a dynamic speaker and coach and is a true professional. I recommend her as a coach, speaker, partner and person; she helps others live the life they only dreamed of."
—C Ward-Wallace, Professional Speaker & Business Coach

"Tiana was asked to speak to a large group of graduate students, who were currently enrolled in several different marketing classes and professors at the University of La Verne. She touched on issues that all were very concerned about how to prepare for future endeavors. She was well received by all and inspired many to ask numerous questions in regards to individual situations. The students felt that the lecture was a big plus in furthering their insight to marketing themselves in the future while pursuing employment. I plan on having her return for the Fall 2012 Semester to speak to an even larger group."
—H Assael, Senior Adjunct Professor at University of La Verne

"Tiana is an amazing coach! Tiana's Professional Coaching Services have catered to my unique, individual development. As a college student, this is very valuable and surpasses the typical services at a campus career center. Overall, Tiana's coaching is effective and it has taught me how to reach success and deal with failure."
—A Barrett, 2012 Graduate UC Irvine, BA Political Science

"I had the pleasure of working with Tiana for a few years and found her to have the ability to solve problems and get things done. She has an incredible ability to manage difficult situations and I was impressed with her performance and I am not easily impressed. Tiana has been very successful and has a proven track record. I believe she has a lot to offer and can be very effective in helping companies and individuals achieve their goals."
—J Medina, CEO Tropical Realty Inc.

"I have had the pleasure of working with Tiana for nearly ten years. I look at her as a total professional bringing insight and understanding to all the projects she works on. I have personally worked with Tiana on getting an idea from fruition to a working conclusion. Her experience and dedication to her clients should be an example to us all."
—D. Solomon, Owner, BDS Natural Products

"Working with Tiana to address my personal and professional goals has been extremely motivating. Having someone to encourage me, who at the same time holds me accountable, has proven very effective. By reciting my self-affirmations daily, and reviewing each of my goals, it takes those goals off the back burner and pushes them into the forefront of my mind...and my goals seem like less of a pipe dream and more of a reality."
—S Lebrun, Stuntwoman, Fitness Expert

Available Programs and Methods of Delivery

Book Signings and Speaking Engagements

Scheduled Book Signings and Speaking Engagements will be booked through contacting ProCoachSpeaks@designingyourpath.com.

Seminars, Webinars, Workshops

Designed to distribute a myriad of topics to large Groups and/or Organizations and facilitated by Subject Matter Experts (SME). Includes topic-specific training material, interactive activities, Breakout sessions, and customized program development.

One-on-One Coaching

Designed for individual development with a personal approach. 2-3 coaching sessions per month are customized for each valued client.

Group Training

Designed for groups of 15 participants for optimal results and participation. Ideal for medium to large-size businesses outsourcing employee training and development. Training includes customized program, Team Building Exercises, Personality Exploration and quarterly follow up.

Customized Program Development

Ideal for small to medium sized organizations utilizing a cost-effective way to train employees. Content is created based on organizational training needs and transferred into a PowerPoint

Presentation. Using Brainshark Software, audio is added to the PowerPoint presentation and shared with staff.

To learn more about Tiana Sanchez Professional Coaching Services and obtain copies of *Undefeatable* visit
www.designingyourpath.com

Tiana Sanchez
International Author
Certified Coach Practitioner
Certified Trainer
Professional Speaker
Strategist

Tiana Sanchez Professional Coaching Services
PO Box 1302
Rancho Cucamonga, CA 91729
Office: 909.703.5989
Email: TianaS@designingyourpath.com

Made in the USA
Columbia, SC
14 August 2024

39955140R00070